Twitter Timeline Advertising

B. Vincent

Published by RWG Publishing, 2021.

TWITTER TIMELINE ADVERTISING

First edition. August 13, 2021.

Written by B. Vincent.

Also by B. Vincent

Affiliate Marketing
Affiliate Marketing
Affiliate Marketing

Standalone
Business Employee Discipline
Affiliate Recruiting
Business Layoffs & Firings
Business and Entrepreneur Guide
Business Remote Workforce
Career Transition
Project Management
Precision Targeting
Professional Development
Strategic Planning
Content Marketing
Imminent List Building
Getting Past GateKeepers
Banner Ads

Bookkeeping
Bridge Pages
Business Acquisition
Business Bogging
Marketing Automation
Better Meetings
Conversion Optimization
Creative Solutions
Employee Recruitment
Startup Capital
Employee Mentoring
Followership
Servant Leadership
Human Resources
Team Building
Freelancing
Funnel Building
Geo Targeting
Goal Setting
Immanent List Building
Lead Generation
Leadership Course
Leadership Transition
LinkedIn Ads
LinkedIn Marketing
Messenger Marketing
New Management
Newsfeed Ads
Search Ads
Online Learning
Sales Webinars

Side Hustles
Twitter Timeline Advertising

Table of Contents

Twitter Timeline Advertising

Welcome to this seminar on timetable promoting. In this course, we will cover how to drive designated traffic from Twitter, with promotions that show up in individuals' Twitter timetables. This course is partitioned into three modules, module one covers crusade targets and subtleties. Module two covers advertisement gatherings and focusing on and module three covers making the real promotion itself and dispatching the mission when this course is finished. You'll realize how to successfully make and dispatch Twitter advertisement lobbies for your business. So right away, how about we jump into the principal module. Alright, folks, welcome to module one. In this module, our master will show you crusade destinations and subtleties. So, prepare to take a few notes and we should directly bounce in.

Twitter Timeline Advertising

Module One

Here. We are on the Twitter dashboard. We will come up here to make crusade speedy, begin once again, and we should discuss these Twitter crusade objectives. Presently crusade objectives or goals you'll see are assuming control over publicizing stages Google advertisement words, Facebook, and a lot of different ones have decided to make this progression in their promotion creation measure, where you can pick normal mission destinations. And afterward those aide you with clues and fitting stations all through the promotion creation measure. We've effectively seen that with a couple of the other large ones. Presently we're seeing it with Twitter and generally, I believe it's certainly great. Unquestionably easier to use. In case you've been doing a portion of these on your own kind of specially appointed in the past that you'll presumably see it's somewhat unique at this point. So, we should discuss application introduces. First application introduces is really basic.

In the event that you have a versatile application, assuming that is your business, and you need to get more individuals to introduce it on their telephone, in a real sense click a connection on Twitter. And afterward that takes them to the application store for your individual, you know, OOS and afterward introduce your application. This is the thing that you're going for. This is your mission objective. The following one is devotees.

Presently it says on and off Twitter here, however clearly the thing we're discussing is measuring your mission accomplishment by the quantity of individuals who wind up after your profile on Twitter. What's more, that is pretty, pretty incredible, particularly if notwithstanding your publicizing, you additionally do a great deal of natural advancement or natural substance on Twitter, and you need to expand the scope of that natural reach. Expanding your adherents with paid promotions is a decent method to do that. Also, tweet commitment. This is a decent one to follow if your essential concern is communication with other Twitter clients on Twitter, assuming you need individuals associating with your image, when you tweet.

So, we're taking a gander at retweets, we're seeing remarks loves something like that. Those will be the thing you're estimating the achievement of these missions. By here, we have advanced video sees. It's quite obvious video, despite the fact that it's not considered as the essential thing on Twitter, since there's, you know, length limitations and stuff is still lovely on Twitter. Furthermore, video advertisements are a, a beautiful huge and effective approach to make yourself clear site snaps or changes. This is likely the most standard issue, you know, basics kind of mission objective. This covers kind of everything, particularly things like lead age, isn't that so? So you really need individuals clicking away from Twitter and approaching your web properties in particular you know, a point of arrival where you're gathering a lead, or then again in case you're doing content promoting, possibly to a substance piece with a retargeting pixel, or on the other hand in case you're selling something straightforwardly, you know, deals pages, internet business stores, item postings, that kind of stuff, the entirety of that will come here.

Also, my speculation is somewhere near 60, 70% of those of you who are watching this video will be depending on this one fairly intensely application re-commitment. So, the application has effectively introduced on their telephone, and you need them to tap on a Twitter advertisement that reminds them to log back in and use it. OK. So in case you're running a some sort of a computer game application for iOS or Android, and this is a decent method to get those individuals to log once again into that application and playing that game with a, with a pleasant, perhaps a video promotion or something, you really see a many individuals doing this, a great deal of organizations doing this current what's that one conflict of factions is doing that kind of thing with advertisements constantly. In transfer video sees, pre-roll this is sounds a ton like, you know, YouTube in transfer video, and that is fundamentally what it is.

You're taking others' substance; you're taking existing substance and you're staying your little video promotion at the earliest reference point of it. It will be quite short, yet you get some lovely cool situation there that you wouldn't in any case get mindfulness. This, you don't actually think often about the retweets. You don't actually think often about snaps to your site. You don't even truly think often about supporters. What you need is your image personality, in a real sense your name, your logo, your character before whatever number eyeballs as could be allowed. Alright? So, this depends on, you know, impressions, regardless of whether individuals are simply swiping by and not actually really aware of the way that they've quite recently seen your image. You're somewhat assembling that subliminal top of brain mindfulness, you know, and this is a decent mission for building that. So presently we should feel free to tap on devotees.

Suppose that we're attempting to fabricate an adherent mission, that we can build our natural reach without paying for promotions on Twitter. Okay. What's more, how it works, this little clarification of how things work. You will elevate your record to fabricate a connected with crowd. You're just paying for the adherents you acquire. So, it doesn't make any difference what sort of commitment you get on this post. We could get, you know, 100 retweets and likes and remarks and all that great stuff snaps to our site, basically anything. What's more, we're not being charged for any of that. Does that, that is all extra, you know, that is all grantees. What we're paying for is simply individuals who click and follow profile on Twitter. So, this is really sweet. In case that is your essential objective, and you have all the fundamental stuff here, you vet your mission's name, you have a beginning date, you have a discretionary end date.

So, we should discuss a few reasons you may have an end date. Suppose you have a business quantity coming up an end date may be helpful. Truth be told, an end date related to sped up conveyance, which will spend your financial plan quicker and attempt to get your promotion before more eyeballs in a more continuous and a speedy manner. Those two things could cooperate very well. In the event that you have a live occasion coming up and real actual live occasion, that is going on a particular day? All things considered, clearly that is had the chance to end eventually ideally a couple of days before the occasion, you know, so that would be a happy chance to use an end, an end date for your mission, just as sped up conveyance. An item dispatch where you've in a real sense just got a multi-day window that would bode well to have a beginning and an end date and perhaps a sped-up conveyance.

OK. be that as it may, a great many people are likely going to allow promotions to run evergreen most brands on Twitter, since it's a piece of their genuine, you know, everyday life, their everyday publicizing. Then, at that point we have, we should see day by day spending plan, and afterward we have all out-spending plan, which is discretionary. So, assuming we need to spend, suppose $25 each day and kind of endlessly, in any case, we need this specific mission to pursue out suppose $2,000, we can arrange it as such. So after anyway numerous days, this will ultimately come to a standstill when we hit our complete financial plan. And afterward we can kind of pause and inhale and glance back at the mission to perceive how it performed and regardless of whether we need to switch things around a tad, start another mission use, you know, an alternate methodology. So that is basically it for crusade subtleties. I'll interfere with this to standard. We will hit next up here and that will carry us to the promotion bunches page. Furthermore, that is the thing that we'll talk about in the following exercise.

Module Two

Hello people, welcome to module two. In this module, our master will cover advertisement gatherings and focusing on. So, prepare to take a few notes and how about we directly bounce in.

So here we are on the advertisement bunch page. Presently the primary thing you'll see is that a portion of these factors appear to struggle with the factors on the mission creation page. Notwithstanding, this is cross-over. Alright. This is somewhat compartmentalization. The thought is you can have different advertisement gatherings. Thus, why not compartmentalize and have one advertisement bunch with one point that closures on a specific day and afterward have the other one with an alternate point takeover on a specific day, all inside a similar mission, same thing goes for spending plan here. You can kind of limit and sub dispense financial plan to a particular promotion bunch inside a mission. In the event that you just need to spend X sum on one showcasing point or one explicit kind of focusing on or something along those, yet at the same time keep it inside one by and large kind of umbrella mission. The following thing here is offered type.

Presently naturally, it's really set to programmed bid. On the off chance that you've gotten your work done, in the event that you have a lovely strong comprehension of the market worth of offers for, you know, the different sorts of commitment or snaps or destinations is that you're going for, on the off chance that you've gotten your work done, target cost can be something that you could join into your mission. Be that as it may, in the event that you haven't and you're new to Twitter promotions, it's ideal. In the event that you just let Twitter and their calculations handle this for you. Presently, we will hit straightaway. This will carry us to our crowd page. This is the place where the wizardry Kevin's. So, our crowd page, the main alternative that you have is on the off chance that you as of now have existing crowds, save the crowd. For instance, suppose you have a retargeting pixel out there and you have Twitter keeping a rundown of individuals who were collaborating with your substance on the web.

You could really fuse these here. We're not going. Socioeconomics, in a perfect world, before you run any advertisement crusade, you ought to have done some economic scientist. You should definitely know who your optimal client symbol depends on a wide range of data. You would take that symbol. And afterward you would utilize these factors here to coordinate with that however much as could be expected. So, age, sexual orientation, where they're found, what sort of innovation they use. What's more, as a rule, in the event that you haven't done that exploration, you should attempt to leave it somewhat wide. Alright. So except if you realize that your item will be more attractive to females either on account of, of presence of mind, you know, in case it's a female related item or you have statistical surveying explicitly that where you really did the investigation and you hit it hard and you discovered that guys are bound to purchase X and females, except if you've done that sort of stuff, you should leave this pretty much wide down here.

You have an odd assortment of various things that you can indicate events. That is clearly beautiful normal. You can pick nations you can limit it down to states, locales, something like that, even postal districts. Notwithstanding, most of these are somewhat uncommon working framework rendition is something that you can focus by in the event that you just need individuals utilizing either working framework, same thing for a gadget model. That is really explicit stages that they're utilizing dialects. That is not really unique. We, we see that sort of thing constantly and even transporters they're versatile transporters. So, relying upon what your advertising, precisely, those may be applicable to you, a great many people presumably will not wind up utilizing these are narrowing somewhere around, by these ones here, however, simply a language and area could prove to be useful for the majority of you.

The following thing here will be the crowd include. This is the place where you get into kind of that Facebook style and narrowing down of individuals by their inclinations, by their past conduct, something like that. So, we could, suppose only for smiles, we're a piano organization. We need to limit by individuals who may be keen on figuring out how to play the piano. As we will go into interests and we will tap on music and radio, and we will discover traditional down here, for instance, and had add, and blast, there you go. We just had around what'd it say, music and radio. It'll give you a gauge on the right-hand side, 381,000 individuals who Twitter has decidedly distinguished as having shown proof of being keen on old style music previously. OK. So that is, that is really amazing approach to target individuals.

Furthermore, as should be obvious, we have a, an objective outline, or a group of people synopsis here on the right-hand side, that changes as you shape and tight your crowd. Presently suggestions are a fascinating one. Essentially Twitter will sort out what the most mainstream hashtags and usernames depend on the crowd that you've chosen. And afterward they will fuse those usernames and hashtags into your promoting for significantly further focusing on. Presently, the issue with that for us is we set the entirety of our socioeconomics to very wide. So, in light of the fact that we're so wide, I don't realize that having Twitter's calculations go out and find well known hashtags and usernames related with this segment will be of any utilization to us whatsoever. So, I'm going to leave that wound down, however unquestionably seems like something worth investigating relying upon how limited your crowd becomes and how tight your socioeconomics get. Presently another new element here is retargeting individuals who saw or draw in with past tweets. That is an immense, incredibly, amazing approach to kind of spend your advertisement dollar on explicitly individuals who are now acquainted with your image. So, you're not getting as much in the method of cold looks, however you're getting some warm crowd too. Whenever we have our crowd, all set up and chose, we will hit straightaway. What's more, that will carry us to the real promotion inventive, which is the thing that we'll cover in the following exercise.

Module Three

Okay, welcome to module three. This module, our master will show you making the real promotion itself and dispatching the mission. So, prepare to take a few notes and we should directly hop in.

Okay. So here we are on the real promotion innovative page. Presently an advertisement in Twitter is a tweet that is imperative to comprehend. What's more, what you can do is venture once more into past existing tweets and transform those into special tweets. Or then again you can simply make one without any preparation. Presently, for our situation, we have one here and you can rearrange incidentally, by natural tweets that you've done in the past booked tweets and advanced just tweets. At this moment, we have a planned tweet that ends up existing. We can use this as our Twitter advertisement, and you truly need to coordinate with your promotion duplicate to what your mission objectives are. So clearly assuming your mission objectives had been site snaps and changes, indeed, you would need some sort of a source of inspiration that prompts individuals clicking and leaving to go to your site.

For our situation, we picked supporters. So, we need an ever-increasing number of supporters. What's more, that fundamentally implies we need individuals to take a gander at our advertisement for a brief period and we need it to address

13

them. We need them to address an inquiry since, supposing that they draw in with our promotion, for instance, by leaving a remark, they'll presumably be bound to hit the follow button too and follow us on Twitter. So that is the manner by which we kind of organized this advertisement here. Presently we should feel free to choose we'll hit straightaway. Gracious, and I should specify clients. Courses of events is the default setting since that is the thing that Twitter is. That resembles 90% of Twitter is the timetable. OK. Be that as it may, you can likewise decide to sneak your advertisements into profile pages and tweet itemized pages, which will leave, chosen to expand our range straightaway. Good. So here we are. We can survey the subtleties of our mission and the advertisement bunch and our crowd focusing on one last season of watchman date.

We have our spending plan, we have our pacing, we have our promotion bunch. We have our crowd here. We have our position that we picked and here is our genuine advertisement. OK. So, a convincing picture that kind of jumps out, in addition to an inquiry our main tune played during specialists and was such and such what was yours. Okay. So ideally, we'll really get a few remarks, a few answers and individuals deciding to follow us on Twitter so we can expand our natural reach. What's more, that is essentially the lone explanation that we're running this promotion, that is our mission. So, we would hit dispatched crusade. Also, there you go. Presently, when your mission is distributed, you will need to consistently screen these details here. OK. You need to keep an eye especially on impressions. So, your general advertisements, your outcomes, which for our situation, indeed, we're searching for follows, alright.

Your outcomes rate, which will be a mix of impressions and results, your expense per advertisement result, which is vital. That is somewhat your primary measurement. That will be a mix of your by and large spend and the outcomes and how that is coordinating toward your day-by-day financial plan. What's more, obviously, watch out for how much cash you have left too. In any case, you will need to change your promotion gatherings and your points etc. In case you're seeing that the exhibition that you're raising here isn't exactly to an acceptable level, and you're not getting your best value for your money out of the spending that you're placing into your promotions. So, ensure you return here, screen your missions, contrast them and one another, contrast them and past information and keep on top of this so you are really getting the outcomes that are best for you for each and every penny that you put into Twitter's pockets. In any case, that is it. Folks. We have effectively gone through the whole interaction now of preparation out, setting up and dispatching our first promotion on Twitter.

Don't miss out!

Visit the website below and you can sign up to receive emails whenever B. Vincent publishes a new book. There's no charge and no obligation.

https://books2read.com/r/B-A-QWUO-WEFRB

BOOKS 2 READ

Connecting independent readers to independent writers.

Also by B. Vincent

Affiliate Marketing
Affiliate Marketing
Affiliate Marketing

Standalone
Business Employee Discipline
Affiliate Recruiting
Business Layoffs & Firings
Business and Entrepreneur Guide
Business Remote Workforce
Career Transition
Project Management
Precision Targeting
Professional Development
Strategic Planning
Content Marketing
Imminent List Building
Getting Past GateKeepers
Banner Ads

Bookkeeping
Bridge Pages
Business Acquisition
Business Bogging
Marketing Automation
Better Meetings
Conversion Optimization
Creative Solutions
Employee Recruitment
Startup Capital
Employee Mentoring
Followership
Servant Leadership
Human Resources
Team Building
Freelancing
Funnel Building
Geo Targeting
Goal Setting
Immanent List Building
Lead Generation
Leadership Course
Leadership Transition
LinkedIn Ads
LinkedIn Marketing
Messenger Marketing
New Management
Newsfeed Ads
Search Ads
Online Learning
Sales Webinars

Side Hustles
Twitter Timeline Advertising

About the Publisher

Accepting manuscripts in the most categories. We love to help people get their words available to the world.

Revival Waves of Glory focus is to provide more options to be published. We do traditional paperbacks, hardcovers, audio books and ebooks all over the world. A traditional royalty-based publisher that offers self-publishing options, Revival Waves provides a very author friendly and transparent publishing process, with President Bill Vincent involved in the full process of your book. Send us your manuscript and we will contact you as soon as possible.

Contact: Bill Vincent at rwgpublishing@yahoo.com www.rwgpublishing.com